EXPLORE THE U.S.A.

DELAWARE

Karen Durrie

LET'S READ

AV²

BY WEIGL™

ADDED VALUE • AUDIO VISUAL

AV² provides enriched content that supplements and complements this book. Weigl's AV² books strive to create inspired learning and engage young minds in a total learning experience.

Your AV² Media Enhanced books come alive with...

Audio
Listen to sections of the book read aloud.

Video
Watch informative video clips.

Embedded Weblinks
Gain additional information for research.

Try This!
Complete activities and hands-on experiments.

Key Words
Study vocabulary, and complete a matching word activity.

Quizzes
Test your knowledge.

Slide Show
View images and captions, and prepare a presentation.

... and much, much more!

Go to **www.av2books.com**, and enter this book's unique code.

BOOK CODE

F486347

AV² by Weigl brings you media enhanced books that support active learning.

Published by AV² by Weigl
350 5th Avenue, 59th Floor
New York, NY 10118
Website: www.av2books.com   www.weigl.com

Library of Congress Cataloging-in-Publication Data

Durrie, Karen.
 Delaware / Karen Durrie.
   p. cm. -- (Explore the U.S.A.)
 Includes bibliographical references and index.
 ISBN 978-1-61913-335-8 (hard cover : alk. paper)
1. Delaware--Juvenile literature. I. Title.
 F164.3.D87 2012
 975.1--dc23
                    2012014759

Printed in the United States of America in North Mankato, Minnesota
1 2 3 4 5 6 7 8 9   16 15 14 13 12

052012
WEP040512

Project Coordinator: Karen Durrie
Art Director: Terry Paulhus

Weigl acknowledges Getty Images as the primary image supplier for this title.

DELAWARE

Contents

3

This is Delaware.
It is called The First State.
Delaware was the first state
to sign the United States Constitution.

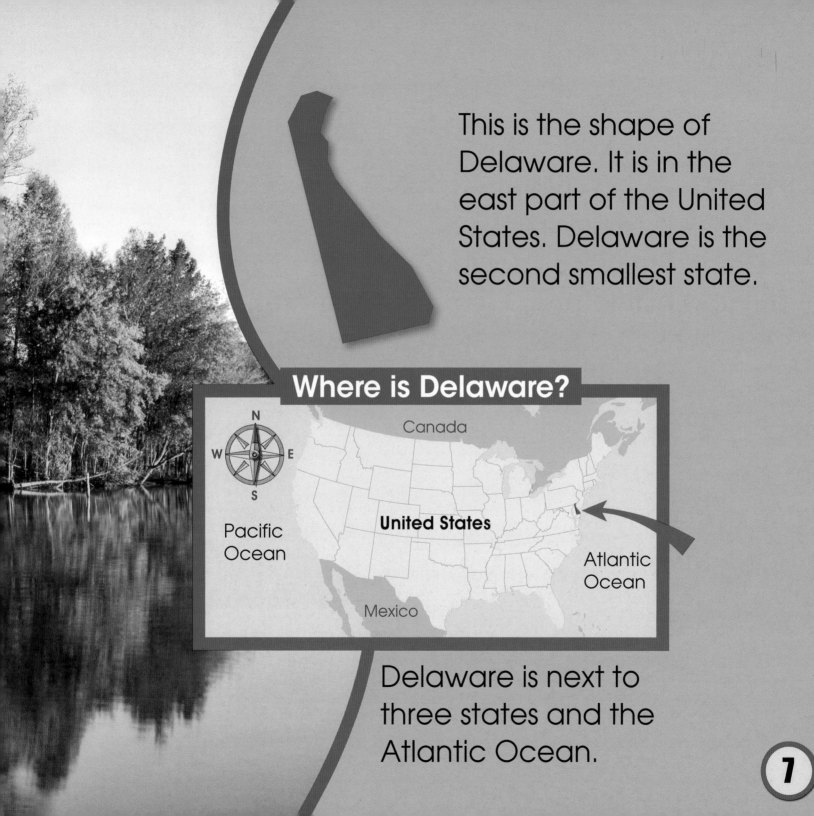

This is the shape of Delaware. It is in the east part of the United States. Delaware is the second smallest state.

Where is Delaware?

Canada

United States

Pacific Ocean

Atlantic Ocean

Mexico

Delaware is next to three states and the Atlantic Ocean.

It is believed the United States flag was first flown in Delaware. It was carried during a battle.

The first United States flag had 13 stars and 13 stripes.

BIRTHPLACE OF OLD GLORY
OPEN TO THE PUBLIC.

The Delaware state flower is the peach blossom. It grows on peach trees. Delaware has many peach trees.

The state seal has two men and a ship.

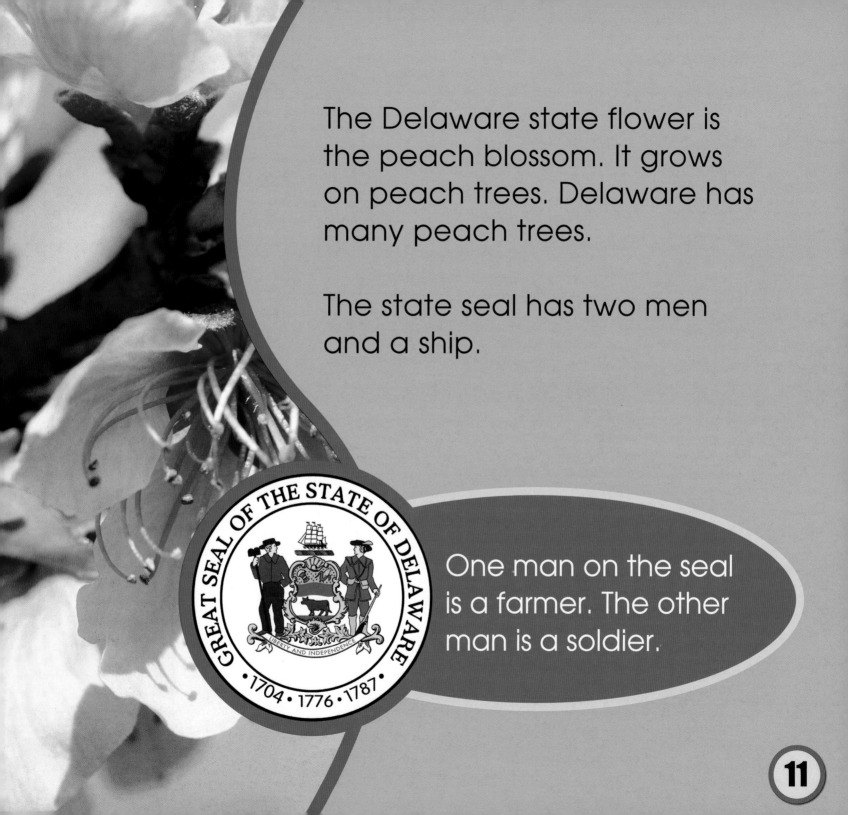

One man on the seal is a farmer. The other man is a soldier.

This is the state flag of Delaware. The flag is blue with a diamond shape in the middle.

DECEMBER 7, 1787

The colors of the flag stand for the uniform of General George Washington.

DECEMBER 7, 1787

We the People

Freedom's First
1787-1987

13

The state animal of Delaware is the gray fox. It is in the same family as the dog. The gray fox can run up to 28 miles an hour.

The gray fox can climb trees.

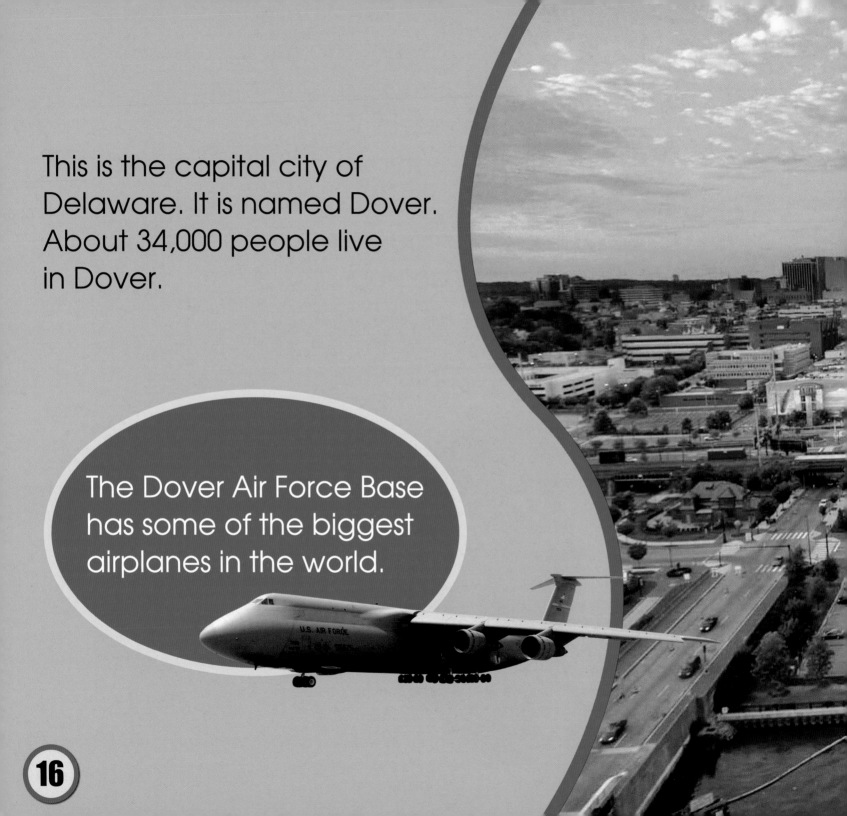

This is the capital city of Delaware. It is named Dover. About 34,000 people live in Dover.

The Dover Air Force Base has some of the biggest airplanes in the world.

Soybeans grow in Delaware.
Foods such as flour, tofu,
and milk are made
from soybeans.

Soybeans can also be
used to make crayons.

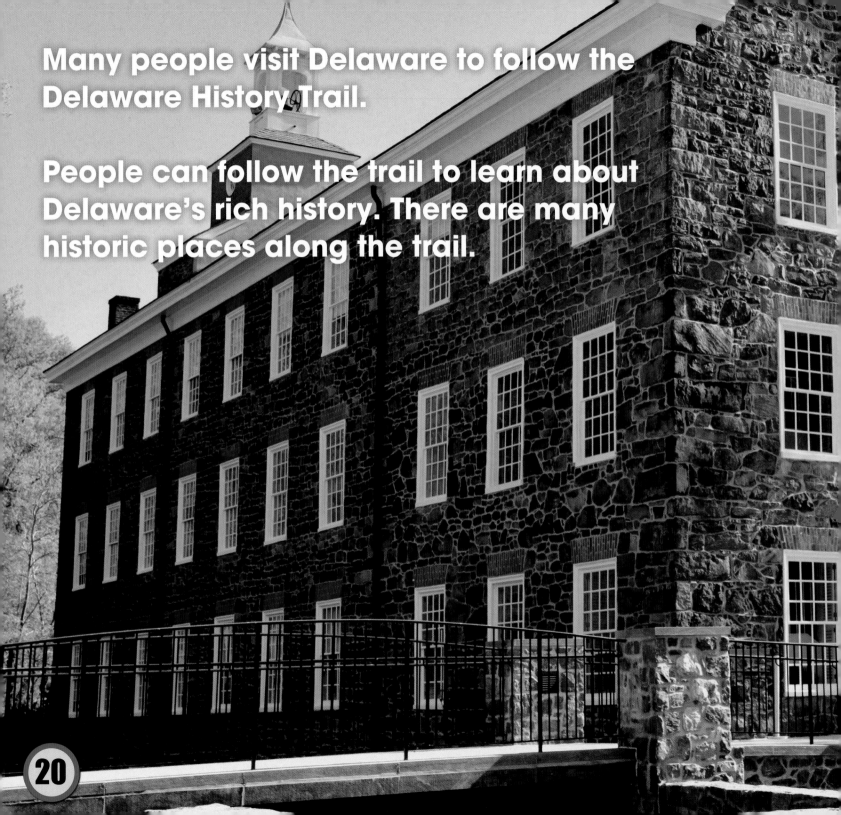

Many people visit Delaware to follow the Delaware History Trail.

People can follow the trail to learn about Delaware's rich history. There are many historic places along the trail.

DELAWARE FACTS

These pages provide detailed information that expands on the interesting facts found in the book. These pages are intended to be used by adults as a learning support to help young readers round out their knowledge of each state in the *Explore the U.S.A.* series.

Pages 4–5

Delaware is called The First State. It was the first of the original 13 colonies to recognize the written U.S. Constitution in 1787. The nickname was not made official until 2002, when a first-grade class lobbied for the nickname. Delaware has three other nicknames. They are the Diamond State, the Hen State, and Small Wonder.

Pages 6–7

On December 7, 1787, Delaware became the first state to join the United States. Delaware borders Maryland, Pennsylvania, and New Jersey. Delaware is 1,982 square miles (5,133 square kilometers), 96 miles (154 kilometers) long, and ranges from 9 to 35 miles (14.5 to 56 km) wide. The population of Delaware is almost 890,000. This ranks Delaware as 45th among the states.

Pages 8–9

The Battle of Cooch's Bridge was the only battle of the American Revolution that took place in Delaware. Fought on September 3, 1777, it is also known as the Battle of Iron Hill. American troops fought British and German forces on the road leading to Cooch's Bridge. The British eventually forced the Americans to retreat to the main continental camp near Wilmington, Delaware.

Pages 10–11

The state seal contains many different symbols. The ship represents the shipping industry. The soldier stands for the revolution that freed the United States from Great Britain. The farmer depicts the importance of agriculture to the state. The original seal was designed in 1777 and updated in 1787 when Delaware became a state.

Pages 12–13

The state flag's colors are called colonial blue and buff. The colors were chosen to represent General George Washington's uniform. The flag also has the Delaware coat of arms in the center. The date at the bottom of the flag refers to the day that Delaware ratified the United States Constitution.

Pages 14–15

Gray foxes are indigenous to Delaware. Gray foxes can run up to 28 miles (45 km) an hour. Fourth-grade students suggested that the gray fox be adopted as the official state animal. The students likened gray foxes to the soldiers at Dover Air Force Base because gray foxes do not hibernate and the soldiers are "always ready."

Pages 16–17

Dover is the Delaware state capital. It was named after a city in England. Dover is the second-largest city in Delaware. Dover Air Force Base, located southeast of Dover, is the largest airfreight terminal operated by the Department of Defense. It can process more than 1,200 tons (1,088 tonnes) of cargo every 24 hours.

Pages 18–19

Soybeans are the second-largest cash crop produced in the United States, after corn. Sussex County, Delaware, is the largest soybean-producing county east of the Appalachian Mountains. Besides many food products, soybeans can also be used to make biodiesel fuel, candles, ink, lubricants, and foam.

Pages 20–21

The 51 sites along the Delaware History Trail showcase the rich cultural heritage of Delaware. The 36 main sites, known as the "Distinctive Dozen," comprise the most important landmarks of Delaware's past. One such building is the Camden Friends Meeting House, which is a worship house built in 1805 by the Quakers.

KEY WORDS

Research has shown that as much as 65 percent of all written material published in English is made up of 300 words. These 300 words cannot be taught using pictures or learned by sounding them out. They must be recognized by sight. This book contains 63 common sight words to help young readers improve their reading fluency and comprehension. This book also teaches young readers several important content words, such as proper nouns. These words are paired with pictures to aid in learning and improve understanding.

Page	Sight Words First Appearance
4	first, is, it, state, the, this, to, was
7	and, in, next, of, part, second, three, where
8	a, had
11	grows, has, man, many, men, on, one, other, trees, two
12	for, with
15	an, animal, as, can, family, miles, only, that, run, same, up
16	about, city, has, live, named, people, some, world
19	also, are, be, foods, from, grow, made, make, such, used
20	along, learn, places, there

Page	Content Words First Appearance
4	Constitution, Delaware, United States
7	Atlantic Ocean, shape
8	battle, flag, stars, stripes
11	farmer, flower, peach blossom, seal, ship, soldier
12	colors, General George Washington, middle, uniform
15	dogs, gray fox, hour
16	Air Force Base, airplanes, Dover
19	crayons, flour, milk, soybeans, tofu
20	Delaware History Trail

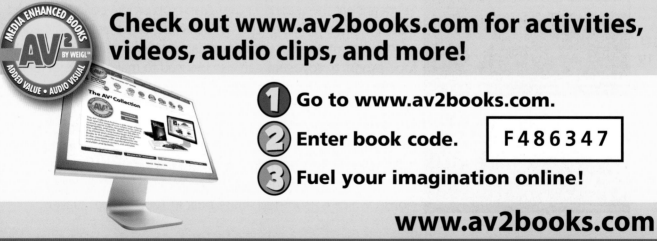